Grand ONE-HAND SOLOS
FOR Piano

8 EARLY INTERMEDIATE PIECES FOR RIGHT OR LEFT HAND ALONE

Melody Bober

Teachers and students occasionally need music for one hand. Over the years, I have had several students who bravely came to their piano lesson after breaking an arm or spraining a finger. This situation offers the unique opportunity to develop the other hand while the injured one is healing.

Grand One-Hand Solos for Piano, Book 4, will allow students to enjoy the musical experience of one-hand playing through vibrant, exciting solos. The pieces in this collection contain music in a variety of keys, styles, meters and tempos designed to help students progress technically and musically. Rhythm, phrasing, articulation and dynamics all become wonderful teaching tools while students master the art of one-hand performance.

I sincerely hope that both teachers and students will find the *Grand One-Hand Solos for Piano* series productive, exciting and fun!

CONTENTS

Alfred Music Publishing Co., Inc.
P.O. Box 10003
Van Nuys, CA 91410-0003
alfred.com

ISBN-10: 0-7390-9275-8
ISBN-13: 978-0-7390-9275-0

Song of Spring Meadow

(for the right hand)

Melody Bober

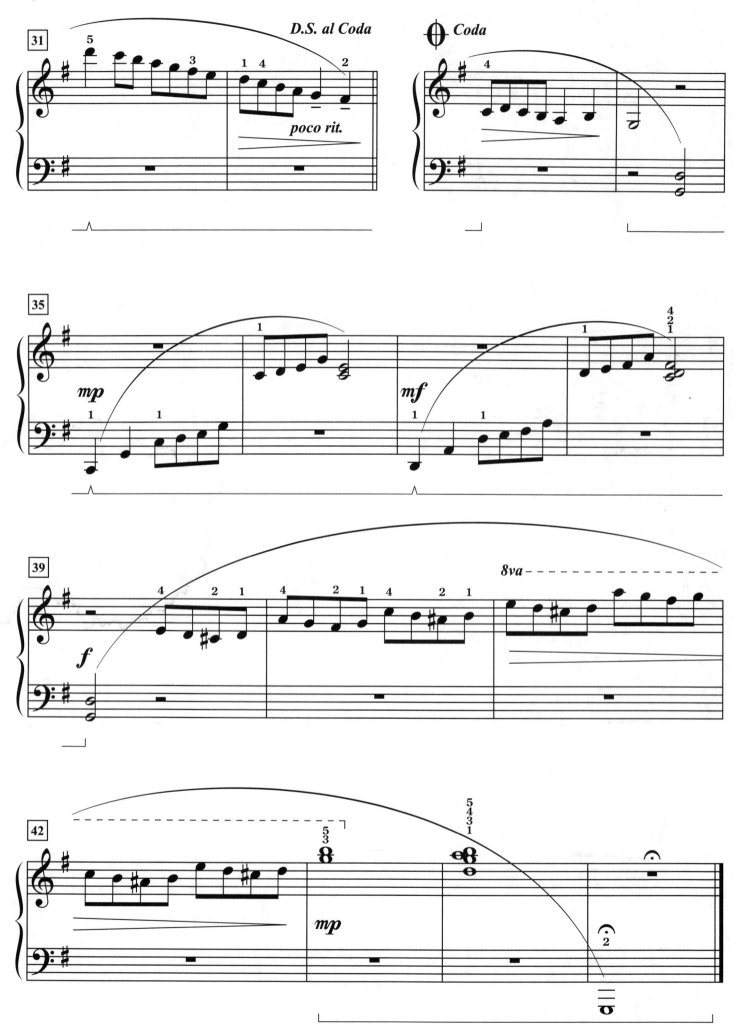

Mystery Mansion

(for the right hand)

Melody Bober

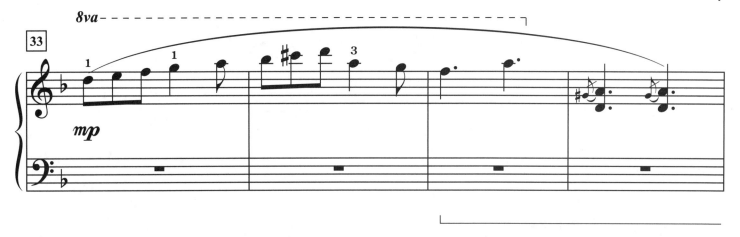

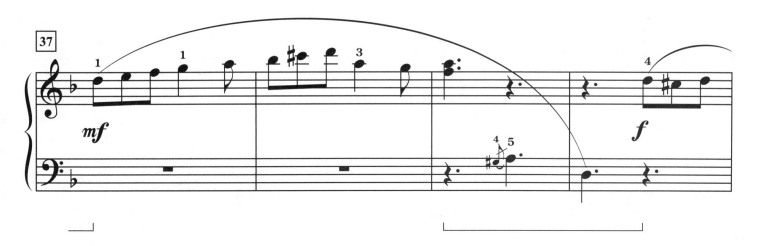

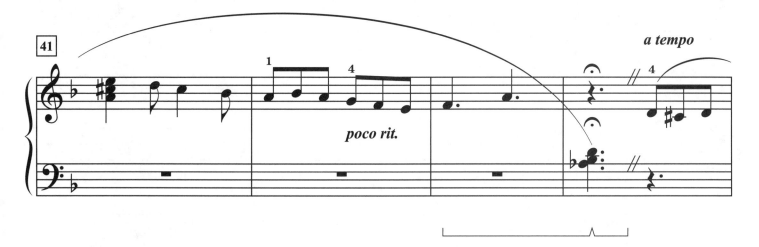

Sleuthing Around

(for the right hand)

Melody Bober

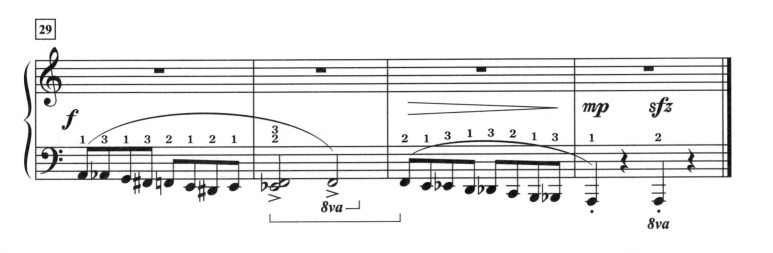

Sunset on Little Pelican Lake

(for the right hand)

Melody Bober

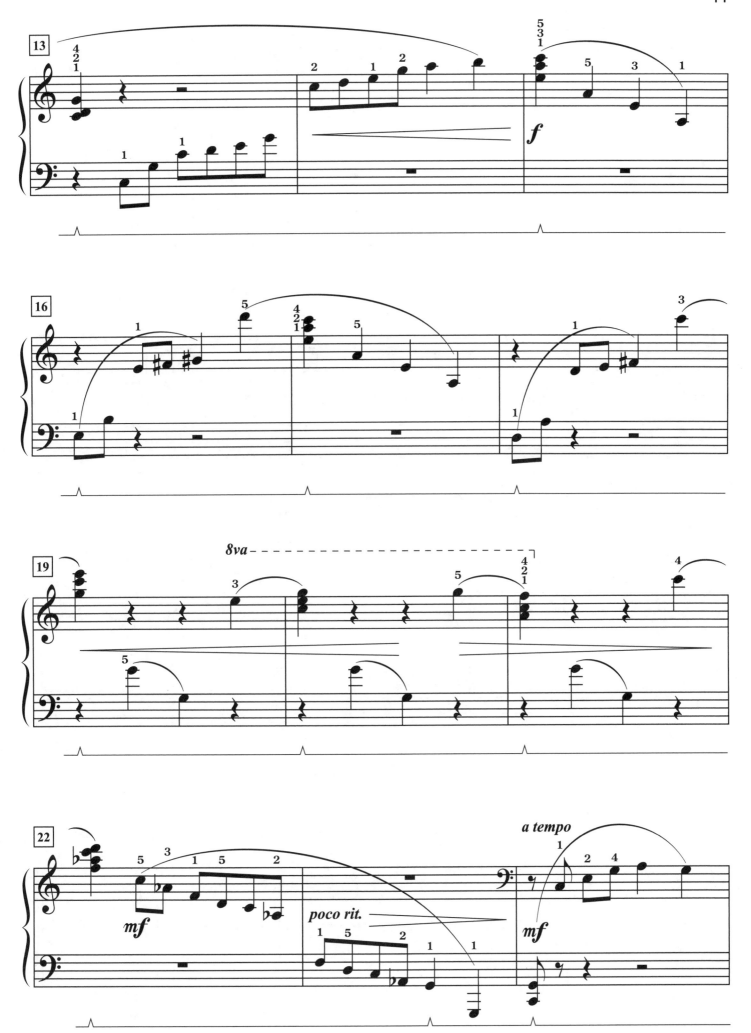

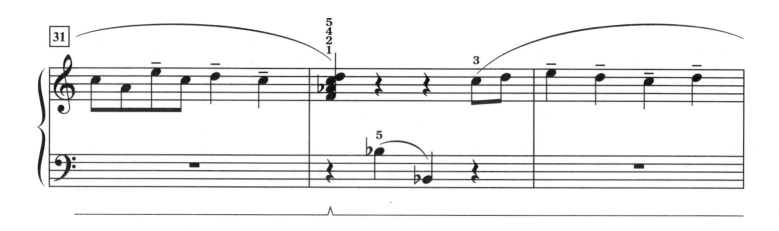

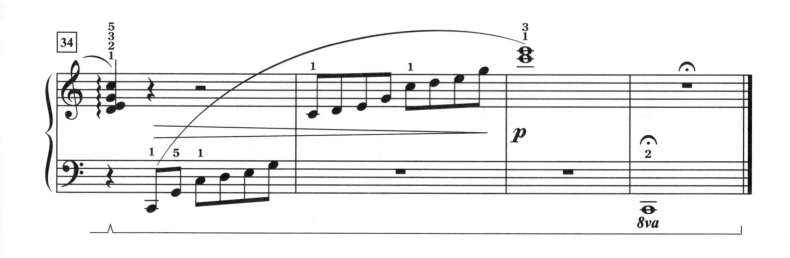

Boogie Blues Riff

(for the left hand)

Melody Bober

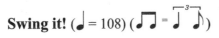

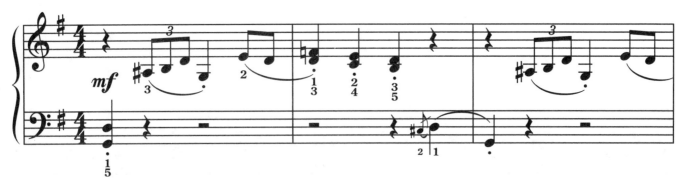

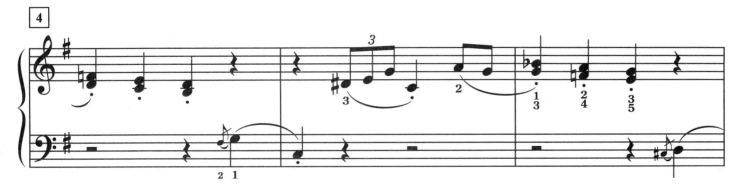

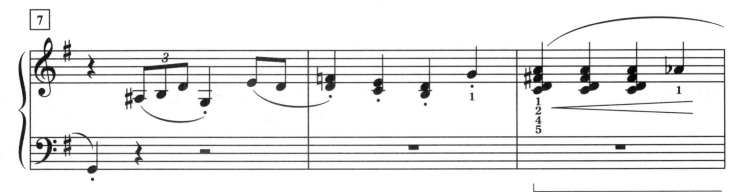

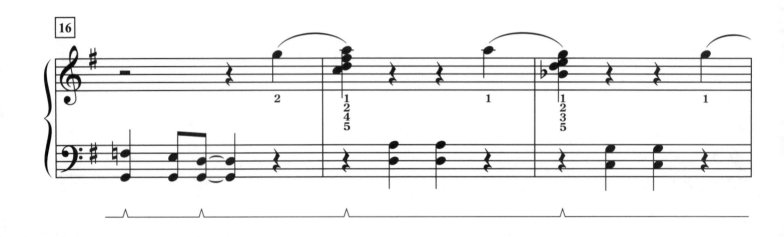

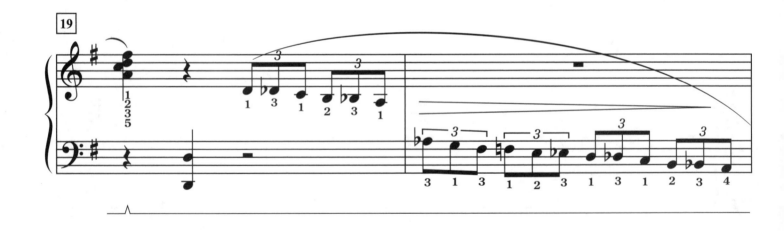

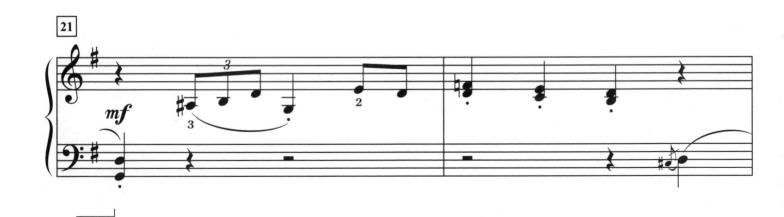

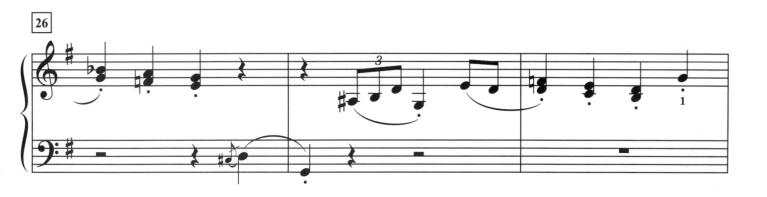

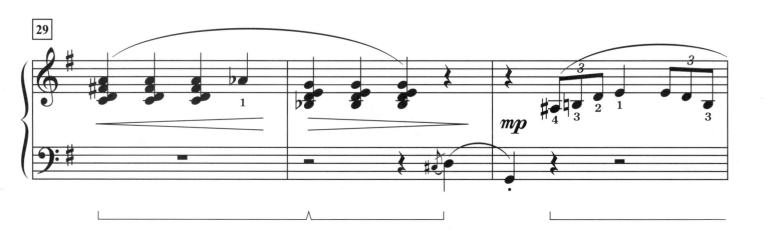

Our Little Waltz

(for the left hand)

Melody Bober

Autumn Wind

(for the left hand)

Melody Bober

Nocturne

(for the left hand)

Melody Bober

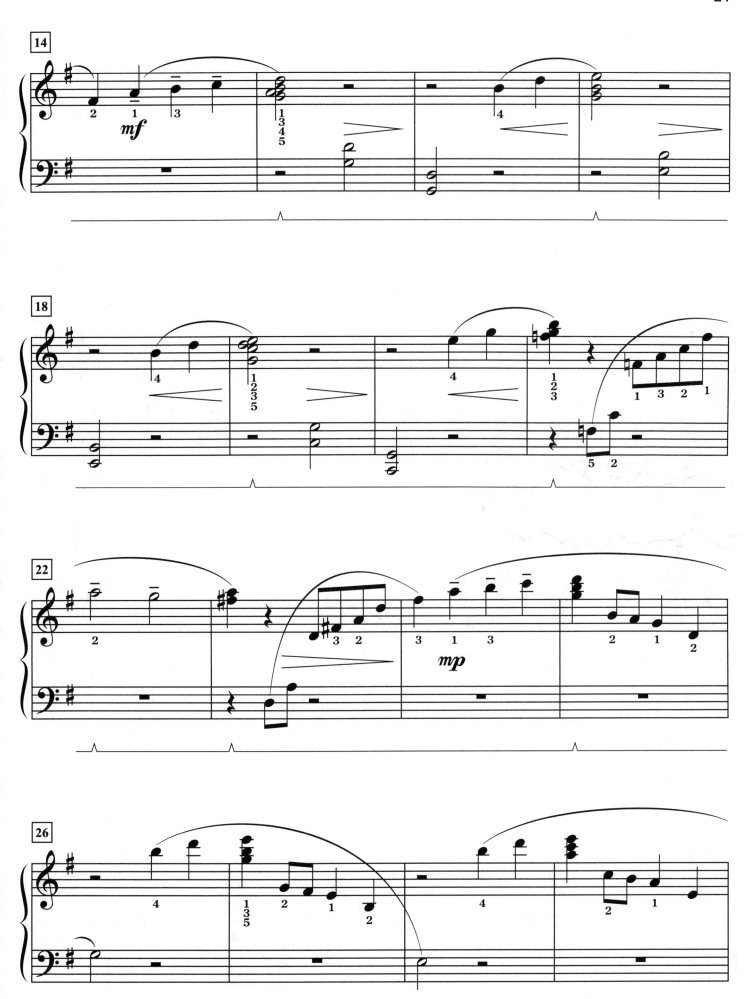

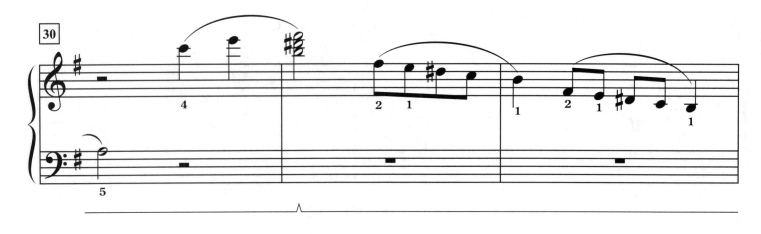

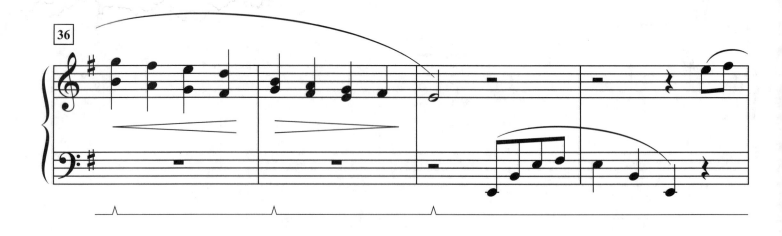